How Do I Become A Christian?

Muriel F. Blackwell

Illustrated by Betty Harper

Broadman & Holman Publishers
Nashville, Tennessee

© Copyright 1990, 2000
Broadman & Holman Publishers
Nashville, Tennessee
All rights reserved.

Printed in the United States
Cover design by Mike Goodson / Goodson Design Group

Scripture taken from the HOLY BIBLE, NEW INTERNATIONAL READER'S VERSION™, Copyright © 1995, 1996, 1998 by International Bible Society. Used by permission of Zondervan Publishing House. All rights reserved.

Holman Bible Publisher's *Read to Me Bible for Kids, NIrV*, is the recommended format for reading the Scriptures to accompany this book.

Library of Congress Cataloging-in-Publication Data

Blackwell, Muriel Fontenot.
　　How do I become a Christian? / by Muriel F. Blackwell ; illustrations by Betty Harper.
　　　p. cm.
　　Originally published: Nashville, Tenn. : Broadman Press, c1990.
　　ISBN 0-8054-2378-8
　　1. Children--Conversion to Christianity. 2. Southern Baptist Convention--Doctrines--Juvenile literature. 3. Christian life--Juvenile literature. [1. Conversion. 2. Baptists. 3. Christian life.] I. Harper, Betty, ill. II. Title.

BV4925 .B53 2000
248.2'4--dc21   00-029252

2 3 4 5 04 03 02

Contents

A Personal Word 4
1. The Bible Is Special 6
2. What It Means to Be Lost 11
3. Jesus, God's Answer for Sin 19
4. Accepting Jesus as My Savior 25
5. You and Your Decision to Trust Jesus 37
6. Joining the Church: The Journey Ahead 42

A Personal Word

Why did I write this book? Because I believe the most important decision you will ever make is to trust Jesus as your Savior. Therefore, I want you to know and understand the following things:

- The Bible is God's message to you; the Bible, God's Word, leads you toward knowing and understanding His love for you.
- What it means to be lost and separated from God's forgiveness.
- God planned for and sent Jesus to be your Savior.
- What you must do to accept Christ as your Savior when God's Holy Spirit leads you to do so.
- What it means to join the church and follow God's will for your life.

As you read this book you will find activities to help you in your journey of discovering where you are in your relationship to Christ. You will need to keep a journal to write down your answers and decisions as you work these activities.

Remember! Making a decision to trust Christ is your own personal decision, which should be made when God's Spirit leads you to do so.

You can do every activity in this book, study and memorize the Bible verses related to salvation, know all the steps one must take to become a Christian, and still not be saved. This book and these activities are to help

A Personal Word

you understand *how* to become a Christian so that you will be ready to make that important decision with assurance when God's Spirit leads you to do so.

"But I'm already a Christian," you say. Fine. Then as you read these pages and take part in the activities, you will be reviewing the things that led you to trust Christ. That should reassure you in what you have done. Because you have already experienced these things, you can even help your friends who are not Christians as they ask questions.

As you read and work through these pages, I want you to know I have already prayed for you. Even though we may not know each other personally, I have asked God to guide every person who uses this book so that he or she will understand how to become a Christian and will make that decision as God's Spirit prompts him or her.

Prayerfully yours,
Muriel Blackwell

A Prayer

Dear God,

Thank You for loving me enough to have a plan for my salvation and well-being in all of life.

Help me to read and study this book carefully and prayerfully so that I may understand how to become a Christian. Also help me to act on that knowledge when You lead me to do so. Amen.

John
John 3
16 "For God So loved the World, that He gave His only begotten Son, that whoever believes in Him Should not perish, but have eternal Life."
NIrV
Read
Me

1
The Bible Is Special

The Bible is God's special message of love because it points the way to salvation for you. The word *special* is used so much in our world today that it has lost much of its meaning. We say we have a special pair of jeans, a game, a friend, or other things. Yet when we speak of the Bible as a special book, it is much more. The Bible should never be put in the same category with things that are temporary like jeans or a game.

The Bible is a book. The word itself means book, but it is far more than just any book. The Bible is the inspired Word of God. This means that God Himself inspired His chosen holy men to record His message for all people. The word *inspired* is not an easy word to understand. That is because it is an *abstract* word.

Abstract means something we cannot touch or see.
It is easier to understand words that are *concrete.*
Concrete words stand for things we can see and touch, like a desk, a ball glove, or a soft drink.

What, then, does it mean when we say that the Bible is the inspired Word of God? It means that God Himself put His message into the minds of the men He chose to write the books of the Bible. God's Spirit led the writers to write His message. God's Spirit also led men to gather these inspired writings into one book, which we call the Bible. It tells you how God loved you enough to send

How Do I Become A Christian?

Jesus to be your Savior. This one central message of the Bible became God's plan for saving all persons. God had a plan from the beginning, and that plan is written in His Word—the Bible.

The Bible Tells Us About God

Probably one of the first Bible verses you may have learned was "God is love." He loves you and wants you to love Him. He loves you so much that He sent Jesus to die for your sins (see John 3:16-17).

God is the giver of life. He created the world and the universe. He created man and woman. When they disobeyed God, sin came into God's world and separated people from Him. However, God is always ready to receive lost persons back to Himself. When we come back to God through His Son, Jesus, God receives us and guides us each day as we allow Him.

God does not leave us without help in our daily lives. Through His Holy Spirit, He goes with us. He helps us do things that honor Him. God teaches us His way, then helps us do it.

God also works through His people. People who have come to know and believe, obey Him through preaching, teaching, praying, witnessing, and ministering. God works through people in the world today just as He did in Bible times. God could do His work without us, but He has chosen to work through us.

The Bible Tells Us About the Old and New Testaments

The Old Testament is a record of the people of Israel and how God chose them to be His special people. He wanted them to share their understanding of God's love with others. The New Testament is a record of how God sent His Son, Jesus, to be the Savior. It tells about those who trusted Him and how they shared the good news of Jesus. It tells how people should live.

The Bible also tells us about Jesus. Jesus came to earth to do God's will. He lived, He taught, He died, and He rose again. Each part of Jesus' work was important. Through His life He showed us how to live as His followers. Through His teachings Jesus helped us know what would please God. He taught about God and about heaven. He showed us the way of salvation and how to live once we have accepted Him. Through His resurrection Jesus brought to all believers the promise of a life in heaven after death. All who accept and follow Christ can have that promise. His work in heaven is to prepare a home for His followers and to represent us to God the Father. Jesus' work also continues on earth today as He goes with each believer in his daily life. He hears us when we pray. He understands when we are sad, hurt, angry, or happy.

The Bible Points the Way to Salvation

The Bible tells us that one who sins is separated from God. Adam and Eve found this out when they chose to disobey God. They were driven from the garden of Eden. They were no longer allowed to live in God's favor.

When a person asks Christ to forgive their sin we say they have a right relationship with God. As you read this book further, you will learn more about words and phrases, such as *sin, repentance, confession, faith, trust,*

How Do I Become A Christian?

new birth, and other terms that are important to becoming a Christian and living as a follower of Jesus.

While the Bible is God's message of love for you, it also points out the sad results of sin and disobedience. The Bible tells us about God's displeasure with His people of Bible times when they sinned, and with us today when we sin. But you can be glad that the central message of God's Word is that He loves you. He wants you to accept that love through Jesus Christ and follow the teachings of the Bible. When you do this, you will go on discovering every day that God's Word is truly a message of love and hope.

Activity

This chapter deals with truths about the Bible that will last forever. Match the Scriptures on the right with the truths on the left. Use the Scripture references to help you. One way to do this is to copy the sentence and the matching reference in your journal.

1. The Bible and its truths will never be destroyed.
2. God's writers of the Bible were inspired by God and led by the Holy Spirit.
3. The Word of God is inspired and helps us know how to live.
4. If you want to learn about God, study the Bible.

A. 2 Peter 1:20-21

B. 2 Timothy 3:16-17

C. John 5:39

D. Isaiah 40:8

Answers: 1) D; 2) A; 3) B; 4) C.

2
What It Means to Be Lost

Terry pulled himself up the steep mountain trail. His face was hot and sweaty. The other boys on the hike were far ahead of him. Mr. Parks, the scoutmaster, called encouragement to Terry from up the trail. Just then Terry spotted an opening to the right. "Ah," he thought, "a shortcut. I'll take this way and catch up with the guys in no time."

An hour later Terry looked around in confusion. The sun had disappeared behind the tall trees and there was no longer any evidence of a trail. And he could no longer hear Mr. Parks calling him. Fear began to take over. "I'm lost," he said aloud. "I'm separated from everyone. Why didn't I stay with the rest of the troop? Don't panic," he cautioned himself. "Remember all the things Mr. Parks taught you about being lost in the woods." Terry sat down and leaned against a tree.

Thirty minutes later Terry heard the voice of his scout leader calling and he answered happily. Terry had stayed in one spot when he realized he was lost and separated from his friends.

The example you have just read points out one kind of being lost, but there is another kind of being lost that is far more serious. This kind of lost is being separated from God who loves and cares for you. This separation comes through sin—making and carrying out deliberate

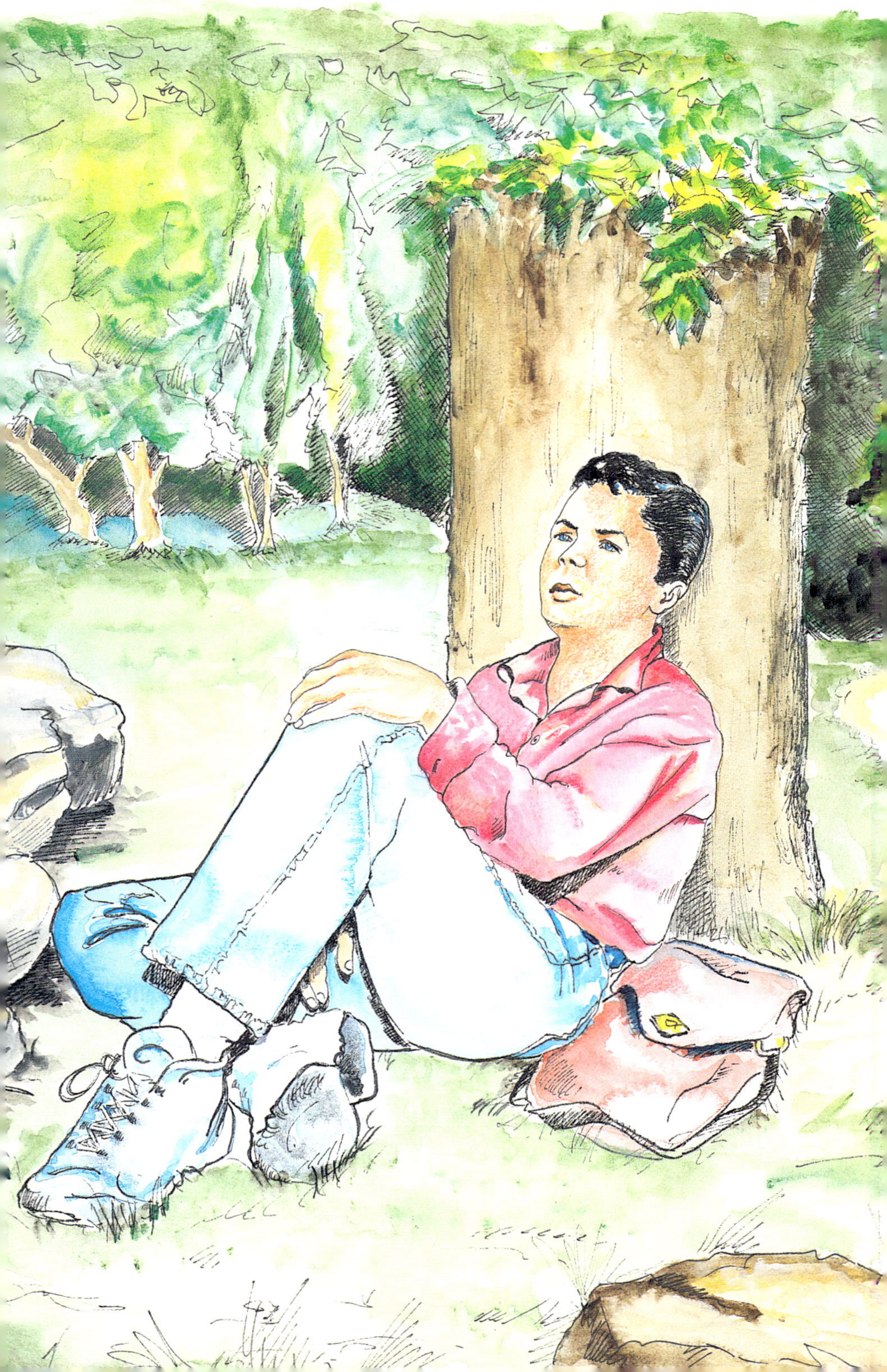

What It Means to Be Lost

decisions to do things, which according to God's rules, are wrong.

When Sin Came into the World

The first book of the Bible, Genesis, tells us how sin came into the perfect world God had created. God formed the first man, Adam, out of the dust of the earth. God then caused Adam to fall into a deep sleep, and as he slept God took a rib from him and made Eve to be his wife and companion.

Imagine how beautiful the garden must have been! God had made Adam and Eve in His own image. He gave them a world that was perfect and beautiful and happy.

There were no troubles, no sin, no sickness, no sorrows, no hurts, and no death. All Adam and Eve had to do was enjoy the place God had given them. The Bible tells us that God Himself came into the garden and walked and talked with Adam and Eve.

God also gave them some instructions. God told Adam and Eve they could eat freely of any tree in the garden except of the tree of the knowledge of good and evil (Genesis 2: 16-17). Because God loved Adam and Eve, he wanted them to know and enjoy that which was beautiful and good. But another event took place in the garden. Satan, the enemy of God, and of all of us, approached Eve. Satan wanted Adam and Eve to disobey God, and he planned very carefully how he could accomplish this.

In Genesis 3 we find the story of how Satan, in the form of a serpent, got Eve to eat some fruit from the tree which God had warned them about. Eve told the

How Do I Become a Christian?

serpent what God had said about the tree, but the serpent replied, "You surely shall not die. God said that because He knows that when you eat it, you will be wise like Him and know what is good and evil."

Eve looked at the tree and saw that it was beautiful. How good the fruit looked! She thought how great it would be to become wise. So she ate and also gave some of the fruit to Adam. Adam and Eve had disobeyed God. They had committed the first sin.

Genesis 3:8 tells us that when Adam and Eve knew that God was coming, they hid from Him. They had made the choice to disobey God, and they knew they had done wrong.

Sin Separates Us from God

The most terrible thing about sin is that it separates us from God. Adam and Eve tried to hide from God. But God knew what had happened. He knew that Satan had deceived Adam and Eve. Since the beginning of the world, Satan has tried to make people disobey God. Being deceived by Satan brought sorrow and suffering to Adam and Eve.

Adam and Eve had to leave the beautiful garden because of their sin. From that point they had to work hard for all they had. But the saddest part of all this was that their sin had separated them from God and all the good things He had done for them.

Pain, sadness, sorrow, and trouble came as a result of sin. Adam and Eve knew that since they had disobeyed God they would someday have to die. But God is a loving God, even when people disobey and disappoint Him. There in the garden of Eden, God made a promise that someday a Savior would come who would save people from their sins.

Sin is present in our world today. From the time sin was committed in the garden, all persons have sinned. Sin still separates us from God and makes people unhappy. Sin is the reason people are lost.

Sin Results in Being Lost

Have you ever heard a person say, "I am really a good person. I try to do what's right. I don't steal, cheat, or harm others. I am not a sinner." That person is wrong. God's Word tells us that everyone has sinned (Romans 3:23).

What is sin? Sin is when a person makes deliberate decisions to do things which he knows are wrong or does not do things he knows are right. Because of sin, a person is separated from God. Until that person asks for forgiveness through Jesus Christ, he is lost. You are lost when you come to the point in your life when you know the difference between right and wrong and deliberately choose to do the wrong things. This knowledge between right and wrong comes at different times in people's lives. When this time comes, we say a person has reached the time of accountability.

Accountability means being personally responsible for your choices and actions.

A person is lost and separated from God until they accept Christ as Savior.

Free to Choose

Just like Adam and Eve, God created all people to have fellowship with Him. When we have a close

How Do I Become a Christian?

fellowship with God, we should love and praise Him. However, He also gave all people who would follow Him the freedom to choose or reject the love He offered them. God did not and does not force anyone to love and worship Him. **Freedom to choose is an important gift from God.**

God has given you thinking and reasoning abilities to help you in your choices. However, with this gift comes the responsibility to make good choices. Everyone must live with the consequences of their choices—good or bad. He also gave you a conscience. Conscience is a deep sense of what is right and what is wrong. Sometimes people abuse their consciences. That is, they do wrong things so much that their consciences no longer help them know right from wrong. Wrong no longer seems wrong. If we respect the conscience God put inside us, this will not happen.

Somewhere from deep inside yourself you know there is such a thing as right and wrong. God Himself put that sense of right and wrong in you. But He also gave you the freedom to make your own decisions. God wants you to make wise decisions based on truths found in the Bible. God's Word can help you understand what is right and wrong.

All people, except Jesus, have chosen the path of disobedience. Sin is disobeying God's teachings and following our own wants and desires. Such actions break fellowship with God, which saddens Him because He created us to love and follow Him.

But God has a plan for bringing us back into fellowship with Him. God's plan provides forgiveness and the opportunity to walk with Him daily. This plan was to

What It Means to Be Lost

send His Son, Jesus Christ, to die on the cross for our sins.

We say Jesus paid for our sins by dying on the cross. We don't have to remain lost if we choose to believe in Jesus as God's Son and trust Him as our Savior. But we do remain lost if we choose not to accept Him.

What, then, does it mean to be lost? It means that one has come to the place of accountability in his life where he knows right from wrong and deliberately chooses to do wrong, or sins, against God.

Activity

Look at the words in bold. Review what you have just read in this chapter. Match the words with the definitions below. You can write these in your journal.

SIN   **REJECT**
CONSCIENCE   **LOST**
CHOOSE   **GOD'S PLAN**
ACCOUNTABILITY

1. Being able to decide for oneself.
2. A time in one's life when he/she is responsible for personal actions.
3. A deep sense of right and wrong.
4. Separated from God through deliberate choice.
5. Deliberate disobedience of God.
6. To turn away from God.
7. A way whereby one may be saved.

How Do I Become a Christian?

Take a Personal Journey

Think about the words and definitions you have just matched. Think about your own life. Where do you think you are in your relationship with God? In your journal write, "Where I Think I Am in My Relationship With God."

When you have completed the activity, share it with a person you feel close to and trust. It may be a friend your own age, a parent, a teacher at church, or your pastor. Ask for help with your answers and for understanding where you are in relationship to God in your life.

Answers: 1) choose, 2) accountability, 3) conscience, 4) lost, 5) sin, 6) reject, 7) God's plan.

3
Jesus, God's Answer for Sin

If this book ended with the last chapter because there was nothing else to tell, how sad life would be. We would always be separated from God without hope. But the loving God did not leave things that way.

God Planned to Send Jesus

God has a plan for you that can make your life one of joy. God wants the best for you. He has given you life. Have you thought about how you will use your life? The first step in using your life for God's plan is to understand your need for Jesus and why God sent Jesus.

The promise God made to send Jesus to be the Savior of the world was made a long time before Jesus was born. Even though people had disobeyed and sinned, God still loved them. God promised that someday a deliverer would come, a deliverer who could overcome the evil in people's lives.

God kept His promise. Jesus came! He came in the form of a tiny baby, who was wrapped in swaddling clothes, and laid in manger. Jesus was born in Bethlehem where Mary and Joseph had gone to pay the taxes required by the Roman government.

Jesus' name was chosen before He was born. Other names for Jesus given by God's prophets were recorded in the Old Testament. The prophets of the Old

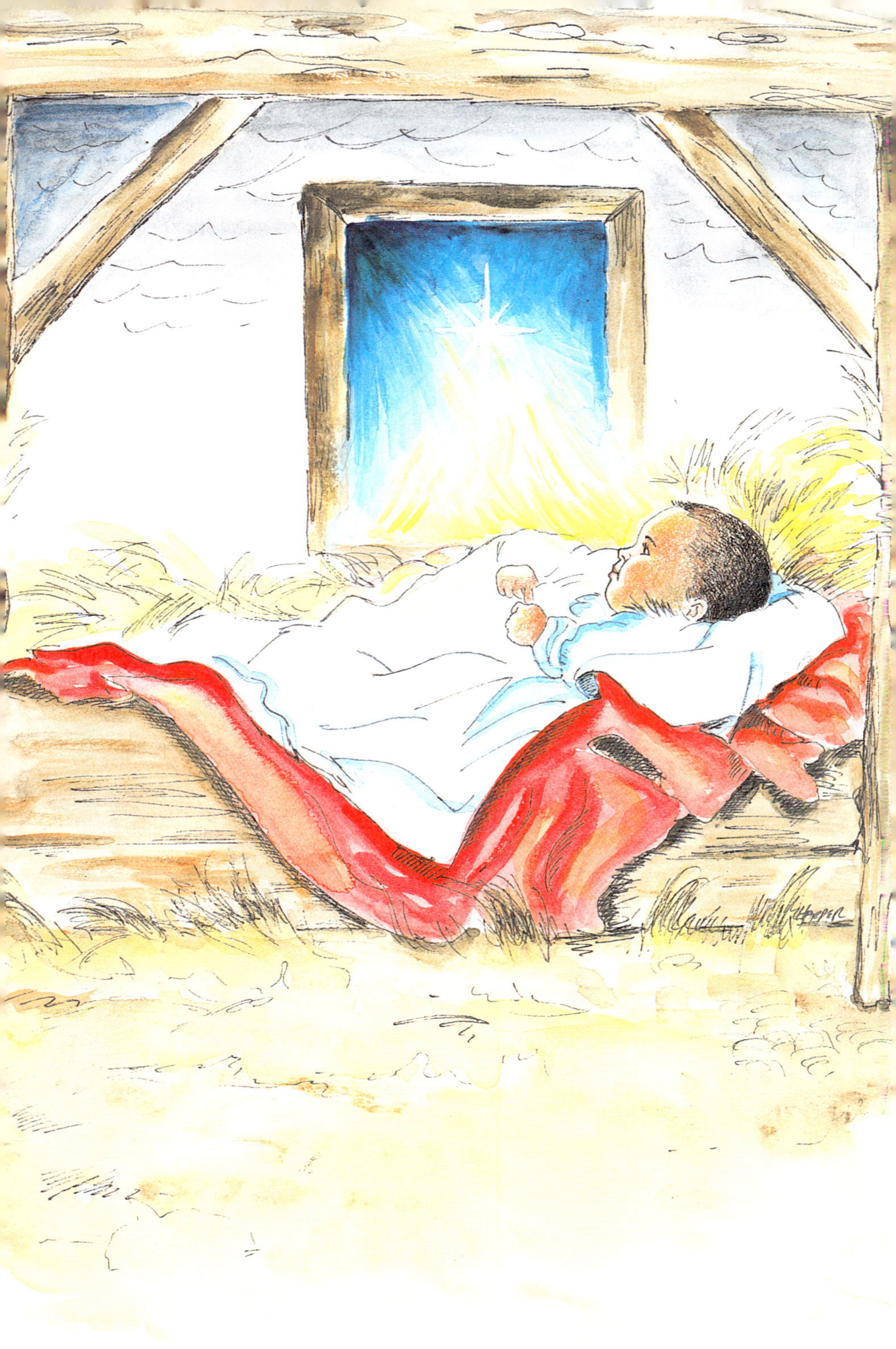

Jesus, God's Answer for Sin

Testament also prophesied or foretold many other things about Jesus, even before He was born. These prophecies were fulfilled and recorded in the New Testament. This is another wonder of God's love and God's plan for the lives of people. These prophecies are in the Bible for us to read and study for ourselves.

The Work of Jesus

God sent Jesus to earth to do important work. He came to live, to teach eternal truths, to die for our sins, and to rise again. Each phase of Jesus' work was important.

Jesus showed us how to live through His own life. How good it is that the Gospel writers (Matthew, Mark, Luke, and John) gave us such vivid pictures of the life of Jesus! His life was the perfect example for every believer who would ever live.

The teachings of Jesus are also important. Jesus told us what would please God. Through His teachings Jesus showed us the way of salvation and the way to a happy life for those who love and trust Him. One of the most important parts of Jesus' teachings was to help us know what God is like.

Here are some of the important things Jesus taught about God.

1. *God is the creator and giver of life.* He created the world, the universe, and man. God continues to create in the world around us. He provides for His creation. He wants to win lost people back to Himself. When persons respond to His love, God guides them through life and prepares a home for them in heaven.

How Do I Become a Christian?

2. *God offers salvation through Jesus Christ.* He offers people a new life in Christ. This life brings such qualities as joy and peace.

3. *God, through His Holy Spirit, is with His followers each day.* He teaches them to do what is right and pleases Him. Through God's help His followers do things that honor Him.

4. *God has chosen to work through His people.* He did so in the Old Testament days. He did so in the New Testament days. And He does so today. As people do such things as read the Bible, preach, teach, and pray, God is working through His followers. The wonderful truth is that God could work without us, but He has chosen to work through us!

Jesus' work went beyond His teachings. Through His death, Jesus redeemed (bought back from sin) all people who love and trust Him. Jesus made an offering of Himself once and for all. He was the sacrifice for sin so that we might come to God through Him.

Another part of God's work through Jesus was His resurrection. Three days after Jesus died on the cross, He rose from the dead and became alive again. This is called the resurrection. Through His resurrection, Jesus conquered death and made a way for His followers. His resurrection pointed out the hope of life after death. Jesus' resurrection gives us assurance that all who follow Christ can have that hope.

Although Jesus returned to heaven after His resurrection, His work on earth continues. Through His Holy Spirit, Jesus goes with each believer in his life day by day. He listens to our prayers. He prepares a place for us in heaven.

Jesus, God's Answer for Sin

Adam and Eve failed God in the beginning. They would not follow the request of God to love and trust Him. People have failed God ever since. God did not want people's lives to be ruined by sin. He had a plan. This plan was to prepare a way through His Son, Jesus Christ. He sent Jesus to be the Savior of all who would accept Him as Savior.

Use your Bible to study the Scriptures on page 24 which point out that God had a plan for loving us and saving us in spite of our disobedience.

Activity

In your journal, write in your own words three or four facts about God's plan for helping you know that He loves you.

How Do I Become a Christian?

The Promise	Old Testament Prophecy	New Testament Prophecy fulfilled
1. The mother of Jesus would be a virgin.	Isaiah 7:14	Matthew 1:18 Luke 1:27 Luke 1:34–35
2. The Messiah would be a descendant of the House of David.	Jeremiah 23:5 Isaiah 11:1	Matthew 1:16–17 Luke 2:4
3. Jesus would be born in Bethlehem.	Micah 5:2	Matthew 2:1
4. Jesus would have power over death.	Isaiah 25:8	Matthew 28:6
5. The Messiah would judge with righteousness.	Isaiah 11:2–4	John 3:16–17
6. Jesus took upon himself our sins so that we could be forgiven.	Isaiah 53:5–6	Luke 23:33–34 1 John 1:9

4
Accepting Jesus as My Savior

Think with me for a few minutes about a scene based on some verses in the Bible (Matthew 27:16, Mark 15:6, Luke 23:18, John 18:40). Barabbas was a robber and a murderer who had laughed at the law. The law had caught up with him, and now he was to be crucified—put to death by being nailed to a cross. Would his companions try to rescue him? Probably not.

After many long hours, the day dawned. Barabbas trembled as he heard footsteps coming toward his cell. As the prison door swung open he heard unbelievable words: "You are free, Barabbas! Jesus of Nazareth is to die in your place."

The soldiers loosened his bonds and Barabbas walked out a free man. What do you suppose Barabbas did? Do you think he was grateful? The Bible does not answer these questions. Surely the least Barabbas could have done was to turn away from his evil life. What would you have done?

Jesus Gave His Life for You

When Jesus was dying on the cross, many things took place. The Gospel writers gave vivid accounts of the crucifixion. During all of His suffering, Jesus loved the people around Him, even the two thieves dying on the crosses beside Him. Surely one of the most difficult

SPORTS
LACROSSE
Baseball
Football
Basketball
Soccer
BIBLE

Accepting Jesus as My Savior

times for Jesus while He was on the cross was the three hours of darkness He endured. The darkness meant that God, His Father, had turned His face away from Jesus. Jesus had taken upon Himself the sins of the whole world—all those who had lived and all who would ever live, including you and me. When God turned His face away from Jesus on the cross, the complete separation from His Father broke the heart of Jesus. In anguish, He cried out, "My God, my God, why have you deserted me?" (Matthew 27:46).

After hours of intense suffering, Jesus died so that anyone who believes in Him will not die but will have eternal life (John 3:16). He gave His life for men and women and boys and girls everywhere. He died on the cross for you.

While He was on the cross, Jesus understood that He was taking on the sin for all people of all future generations, even for you and me.

We are all sinners. We make deliberate decisions every day to disobey God's rules for living. This is sin, and it separates us from God. But God has given us a way to be united with Him, by accepting Jesus into our heart.

Becoming a Christian

You have probably heard many things about becoming a Christian, especially if you attend church regularly. You study from your Bible and church materials about being saved. You hear the pastor preach from the pulpit about "giving your heart and life to Jesus." You hear other people use words and phrases related to being converted. You may not understand many of these words. Remember in the first chapter of this book we

How Do I Become a Christian?

talked about *abstract* words and *concrete* words? (Review those word meanings found on page 6.)

Let's look at some *abstract* words or phrases we often hear related to becoming a Christian. Which words or phrases have you heard or read?

- give your heart to Jesus
- being saved
- being converted
- becoming a Christian
- the new birth
- entering the kingdom of heaven
- trust Jesus as Savior
- turn away from sin
- being born again
- salvation
- repentance
- lost

Are there other words and phrases you have heard which are hard to understand? Write them in your journal and ask someone to help you understand them.

It is important to remember that you won't ever completely understand all the things related to salvation. No one understands all the wonders of being saved. However, you will come to know and understand what is necessary to be saved. This will come as you read the Bible and study at church. You will learn as you listen to your pastor and your Sunday school teacher. You will understand more as you ask questions and pray. God's Holy Spirit will help you in this process.

Understanding the Necessary Things

The Bible gives us many verses related to salvation and being saved. Here are just a few to help you better understand what is necessary to become a Christian. After you become a Christian, you will want to continue to study the Bible and learn more about what it means to follow God's plan for your life.

To become a Christian, you must recognize and acknowledge some things. Read the following facts carefully.

Every person has sinned. "Everyone has sinned. No one measures up to God's glory" (Romans 3:23).

Sin separates us from God. "When you sin, the pay you get is death. But God gives you the gift of eternal life because of what Christ Jesus our Lord has done" (Romans 6:23).

To become a Christian a person must also *repent of sin.* "What I'm about to tell you is true. No one can see God's kingdom without being born again" (John 3:3).

Believe in Jesus. "Anyone who believes in the Son has eternal life. Anyone who says no to the Son will not have life. God's anger remains on him" (John 3:36).

Confess his faith. "Say with your mouth, 'Jesus is Lord.' Believe in your heart that God raised him from the dead. Then you will be saved" (Romans 10:9).

In earlier chapters of this book we talked about:

- how sin came into God's perfect world.
- the Bible is God's inspired message of love for us.
- what it means to be lost.
- Jesus was God's plan for bringing us back to Himself.

How Do I Become a Christian?

Now we are talking about you making a decision to trust Jesus based on a better understanding of these important things. Of course that decision should come only as God's Holy Spirit leads you to do so.

There are three important actions or steps you need to follow in becoming a Christian.

1. *Repent of Sin*

Repent means to be sorry for doing a thing, and that you will try never to repeat it. Repentance is feeling sorry for sinning and having a great desire to turn in the opposite direction. When a person repents, he changes both his mind and his heart.

Of course, people who have repented sin again. No person is perfect. But one who loves Jesus is sorry when he sins. A true follower of Jesus tries not to sin.

2. *Believe in Jesus*

To believe in Jesus means to trust Jesus. This means that you believe that Jesus is the Son of God and that you are trusting Him to save you from your sins. Because of Jesus' life, death, and resurrection, you can have forgiveness for your sin. God sent Jesus to offer salvation to you.

3. *Confess Your Faith*

Just as repentance is turning *away* from something, faith means turning *toward* something. When we repent, we turn from sin. When we show faith, we turn toward God and His forgiveness.

Another way to look at faith is to say that we have complete confidence in God. Faith is to trust in all the truths of the Bible and what the Bible tells us about God. Even though we do not *understand* all the things in the Bible, when we have faith we know that those things are true. We accept for ourselves the truth of God personally.

Accepting Jesus as My Savior

"How can that be?" you may ask. We do not fully know. But when God's Spirit impresses your mind and heart in this matter of salvation, and you follow His leadership, you too will know the peace and assurance that faith brings.

The New Birth

In the world today we hear a lot about "born-again Christians." Sometimes we see and hear people give testimonies about being "born again." These words are difficult to understand. Nicodemus, an important man of the New Testament, asked Jesus to explain to him what it means to be "born again" (John 3:7b).

Jesus said, "No one can see God's kingdom without being born again" (John 3:3a).

Jesus explained that a person is born physically of human parents, but there is also a spiritual birth that needs to happen to a person. God's Spirit can change a person so that they want to live as God wants them to.

Jesus explained to Nicodemus that you can't see what causes the change, but you can feel the difference it makes in your life. You want to follow God and do the things your heavenly Father wants you to do. It is like the wind. You can feel the wind blowing, but you don't know where it comes from. If you want to be a part of God's kingdom, you must believe in God's Son. Then you can live with God forever.

John wrote about the meeting Jesus had with Nicodemus. The important truths Jesus shared are summed up in John 3:16. Find that reference in your Bible and read it again.

How Do I Become a Christian?

You and the New Birth

When you were born, you entered a physical world with a physical body. As you entered this physical world, you breathed the breath of your new surroundings into your lungs.

When you are saved from sin, you are born into the kingdom of heaven, which is a spiritual world. You are born not physically, but spiritually. When you accept Christ and experience this new birth, God's Holy Spirit makes you alive to spiritual things.

A person who has been born again has a new nature. He is a different kind of person—one who wants to live for and please God.

Let's Summarize!
- Repentance is turning away from sin.
- Believing in Jesus is trusting Him to save us.
- Faith is turning to God.
- New birth is God remaking us spiritually.

When you accept Jesus as Savior, God no longer looks on you as being separated from Him by sin. You have trusted God's plan for bringing you unto Himself. God looks at you through your trust in His Son, and He forgives your past sins. He is willing to forgive you when you sin again. He also strengthens you and helps you as you try not to sin.

The Full Circle of Trust

The Bible helps you know how to become a Christian. Many verses in the Bible deal with salvation. Now it's time for you to discover some things on your own. Look at the circle on page 34. There are six questions on the next page, one for each segment of the circle.

Accepting Jesus as My Savior

Read each question and use your Bible to help you answer the questions in your own words. Write your answers in your journal.

1. Why do I need to become a Christian? (Romans 3:23).
2. What did God do because of His love for me to keep me from being separated from Him? (1 John 4:14)
3. What must I be willing to do to have Jesus as my Savior? (1 John 1:9, Acts 16:31).
4. How is a person saved? (Ephesians 2:8).
5. When I accept Jesus as my Savior and become a Christian, what is God's gift to me? (Romans 6:23).
6. Where am I now in my journey to become a Christian?

The *full* circle of trust becomes complete when you can answer question number six something like this: "I have trusted Jesus to save me because I understand my need for Him and how to trust Him. God's Holy Spirit led me to this decision. Other people in my life also helped me come to this decision."

Accepting Jesus as My Savior

The Bible Helps Me Know

Some important words related to accepting Jesus are:

Savior	*save*	*sins*
lost	*repent*	*gospel*
loved	*believe*	*confess*

Read carefully the Bible verses on page 36. The words listed above are underlined with the proper definitions in the second column on the next page. Read the Scripture references and match them with the correct definition. These words and definitions should help you to better understand salvation through Jesus Christ.

The activity on page 36 is adapted from *Children's Bible Study, OND, 1988.* ©Copyright, LifeWay Christian Resources of the Southern Baptist Convention.

How Do I Become a Christian?

1. "Today in the town of David a <u>Savior</u> has been born to you. He is Christ the Lord" (Luke 2:11).

2. "You must give him the name Jesus. That is because he will <u>save</u> his people from their <u>sins</u>" (Matthew 1:21).

3. "The Son of Man came to look for the <u>lost</u> and save them" (Luke 19:10).

4. "(<u>Repent</u>) (of) your sins and believe the <u>good news</u>" (Mark 1:15).

5. "God <u>loved</u> the world so much that he gave his one and only Son. Anyone who <u>believes</u> in him will not die but will have eternal life" (John 3:16).

6. "What about someone who (<u>confesses</u>) in front of others that he knows me? I will also say in front of my Father who is in heaven that I know him" (Matthew 10:32).

A. The good news of what God has done for us through Jesus' life, death, and resurrection.

B. To tell God that you have sinned and that you are trusting in Jesus. Then to tell others that you believe in Jesus.

C. One who saves from danger. A name for Jesus.

D. God loves us so much that He sent Jesus to be our Savior.

E. Choosing your way instead of God's way. Doing things that displease God.

F. Jesus rescues from sin those who have trusted Him.

G. To trust Jesus to forgive you and to promise to live for Jesus.

H. To tell God you have not followed His way. To be sorry for doing wrong things and to never want to do them again.

I. Separated from God because of sin.

Answers: 1) C; 2) F, E; 3) I; 4) H, A; 5) D, G; 6) B

5
You and Your Decision to Trust Jesus

You and I have become partners as we have walked through the pages of this book together. We have looked at important ideas and promises. These will help you understand how to make the most important decision of your life—to trust Christ as your Savior and follow Him.

Perhaps you have already made a decision to trust Christ. Or, perhaps you believe that it is time for you to trust Christ. With your Bible, a pencil, your journal, and this book, find a quiet place where you can read, think, pray, study your Bible, and write down some thoughts of your own. Use the following suggestions during your quiet time with God.

Remember! God Planned for Jesus, the Savior

"The Father has sent his Son to be the Savior of the world" (1 John 4:14).

"Who is Jesus?" you might ask. Let's think about that. Review these facts carefully. They are keys in God's plan to provide salvation for everyone.

- From the time Adam and Eve chose to disobey God (sinned), all people have chosen to sin.
- God worked out His plan for saving people until it was time for Jesus to be born.

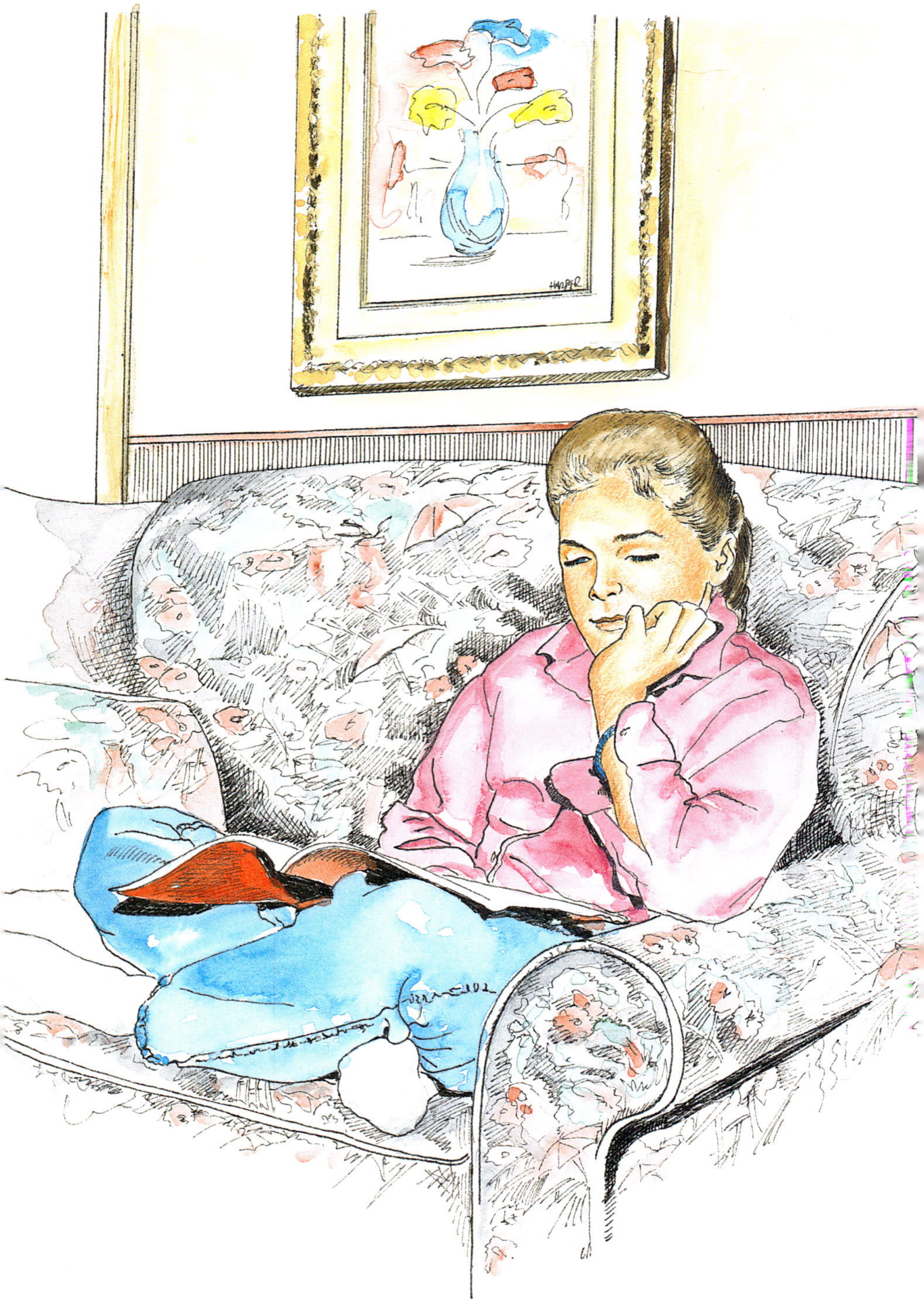

You and Your Decision to Trust Jesus

- Jesus had to die on a cross in order for people to have forgiveness for their sins.
- Even though Jesus died on a cross, He arose and is alive today.
- Jesus is ready to forgive persons who repent, confess their sins, and believe in Him.

Remember! You are Responsible for Your Choices

Study the following chart. Read each Bible verse prayerfully. Think about each word in the first column and its definition in the second column.

Accepting Jesus As My Savior

1. *Conviction* (John 3:6; Romans 3:23; Romans 6:23) — Becoming aware of a great need for God; to realize that I am separated from God and lost because of sin.

2. *Repentance* (Acts 3:19; Acts 2:38) — Being very sorry for the wrong things I do—the sins I commit; wanting to be forgiven and not to sin against God.

3. *Faith and Surrender* (Romans 10:9; Ephesians 2:8; Hebrews 11:6) — Trusting God for His forgiveness; giving God control of my life.

4. *Forgiveness and Salvation* (1 John 1:9; Acts 16:31; Ephesians 2:9) — Being pardoned and saved from my sins by accepting Jesus through God's mercy and love.

5. *Living and Sharing My Faith* (Proverbs 20:11; Ephesians 2:10; 2 Timothy 2:15) — Doing God's will; obeying His teachings; seeking to help others know about God's love.

How Do I Become a Christian?

What Is My Next Step?

Perhaps you should talk with your parents, Sunday School teacher, or your pastor for better understanding. The important decision to trust Jesus as your Savior is a very personal decision. No one can make that decision for you. No one should tell you when to make that decision. This is a matter between you and God. True, the adults in your life can help you better understand about salvation, but they cannot make your decision for you. Nor should you make decisions about salvation just to please another person. Such a decision should come when you know that God is speaking to you through His Holy Spirit. When the Holy Spirit works in your mind and heart you will know it. God will help you to respond and make the right decision.

Activity

Read the following questions. You might want to write down your answers in your journal.

1. Why do you think the Bible is God's message of love for you?
2. Put into your own words what it means to be lost.
3. State in one or two sentences what God's plan is for saving the lost.
4. Review Chapter 4, "Accepting Jesus as My Savior." Then list the important steps you must take to trust Jesus as your Savior.
5. Pray a prayer of thanks to God for providing a way of salvation. After your thank-you prayer, decide what your next steps are in the important

You and Your Decision to Trust Jesus

matter of trusting Christ. Write your decision down.
6. Now decide on a trusted adult in your life with whom you will share your feelings and questions about your next step. Write that person's name and why you chose him or her.
7. Share with that adult. Follow through on your decision for the next steps you need to take, as God leads you to do so.
8. Write down what you have done related to the first seven suggestions.
9. When you have trusted Christ as Savior, write down your thoughts and feelings in your journal. Some things you might include are: the date, your age, persons who helped you understand how to make your decision, how and where you made this decision, and how you feel about it. This personal account will always be a reminder to you of this important time in your life.

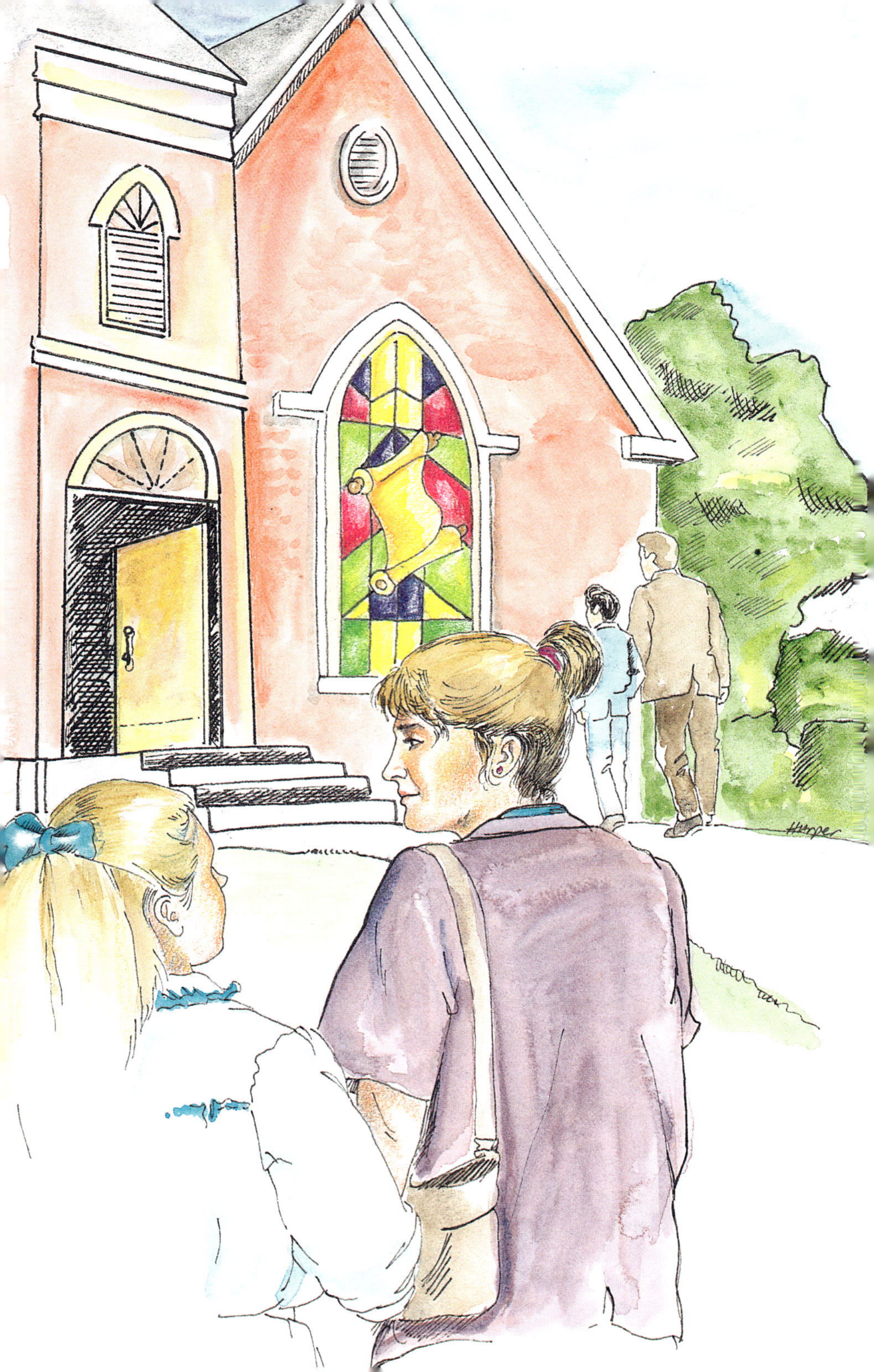

6
Joining the Church: The Journey Ahead

The Church is Special

The church is special. It was special even during New Testament times. In Ephesians 5:25 we find these words: ". . . Christ loved the church. He gave himself up for her."

The word *church* is a special word. In the New Testament the word means "people who are called out." "Called out where?" you may ask. Called out in this sense means "set apart" from the world around them. The people of the New Testament church were different because they were followers of Jesus. They had believed and accepted that He was the Messiah. Therefore, they joined themselves together to worship, to praise, and to share the message of Christ with all the world.

The word *church* is used to describe the building where people worship. Still others use the word *church* to mean the actual worship services. The church is certainly all of these and even more. Probably the best definition of the word *church* is **people who have believed in Jesus, who have been baptized, and who come together to worship and serve God.**

The church, then, is people—not a building, and not just a worship service.

How Do I Become a Christian?

Who Can Be a Church Member?

There are many different beliefs about who can be a church member and when one can become a church member. In a Baptist church a person needs to do two things to become a member.

1. A person must first accept Jesus as Savior and Lord. When an individual has made this decision, they share the decision with the church. This is called "making a profession of faith" and tells the church that they have trusted Christ as Savior.
2. They are baptized. Once a person has accepted Jesus, made a profession of faith, and is baptized, they are then a member of the church.

Only those persons who have trusted Jesus as Savior should join the church. Joining a church does not save anyone. Joining the church should come only after a person has trusted Christ.

You, Personally

As soon as you trust your life to Christ, you will want to make a public profession of faith. That is, you will want other people to know that you have made a decision to follow Christ. Your salvation doesn't come when you make a public profession of faith. Your salvation comes the moment you believe and trust Christ. You join the church *because you are* a Christian, not *in order to become* a Christian.

When you accept and trust Christ as your Savior, you will want to join the church because you want to live for Him. You will want other Christians to know of

Joining the Church: The Journey Ahead

your decision. You will want to join with other Christians to live the way Christ taught and to share the message of Christ with other people.

Baptism is the way into church membership. When a saved person is baptized in the church, they become a member of that church. Only a person who has come to the time of accountability in his life and trusted Jesus as Savior should be baptized. (Remember Chapter 2 discussed accountability and freedom to choose.)

Jesus told His disciples to make believers first and then to baptize them. These instructions from Jesus were given in Matthew 28:19-20.

You have probably read and heard about the baptism of Jesus. Jesus was without sin, yet He asked John the Baptist to baptize Him so that He could set an example for us. This beautiful scene is recorded in the third chapter of Matthew.

When you are baptized you will be following the example of Jesus. You will be confessing to all the world that you have freely chosen to follow Jesus.

Through your baptism you will be following Jesus in obedience and love. You will begin a life of friendship with and service to Him. The central truth of the Christian faith is loving and following Jesus.

Responsibility

Being a member of Christ's church is a unique honor and privilege. But along with the privilege and honor comes responsibility. Each church member is responsible. Adults have some responsibilities. Young people have some responsibilities. And children who are members have some responsibilities.

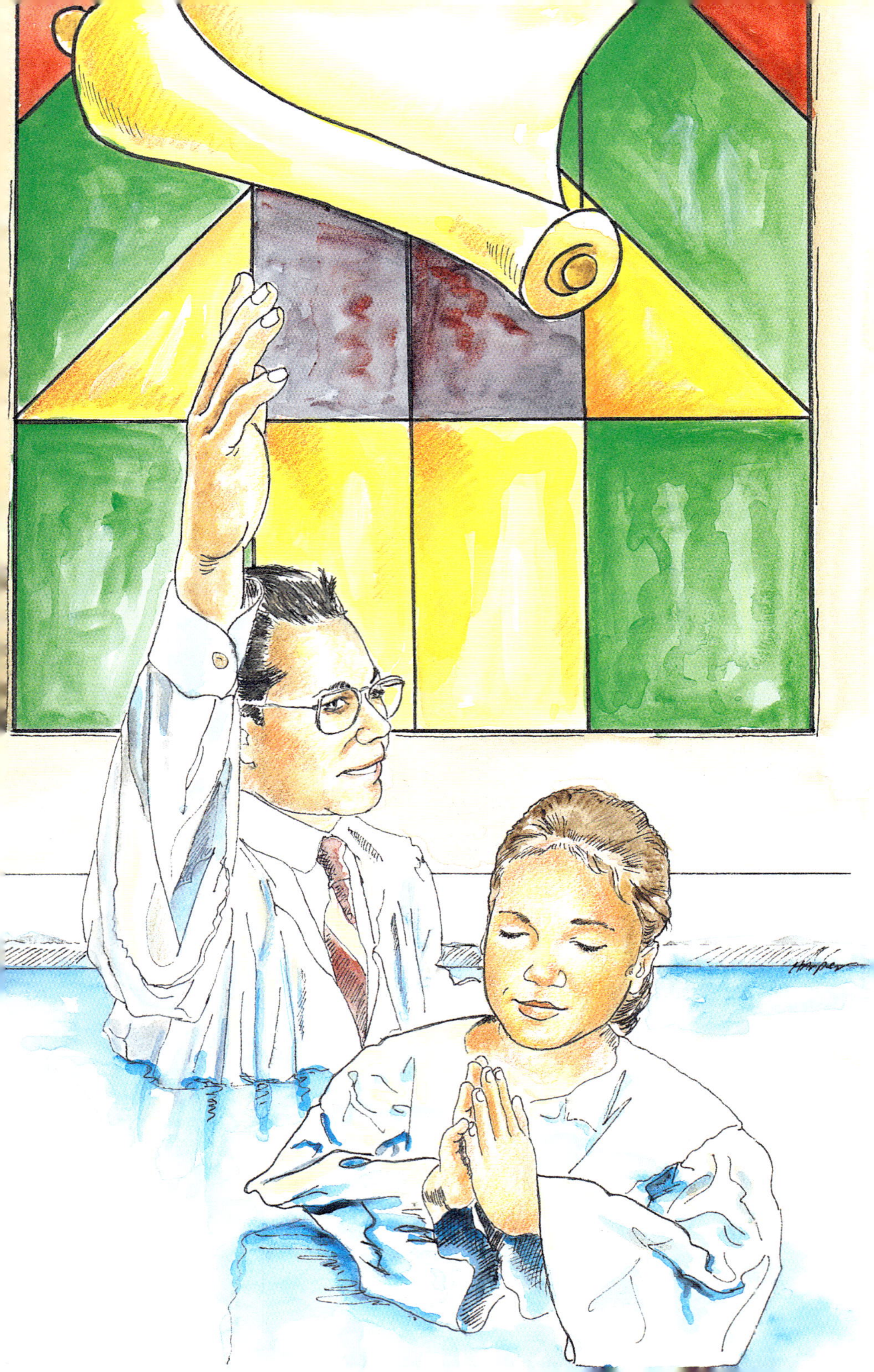

Joining the Church: The Journey Ahead

If you trusted Christ for salvation and joined the church, you have responsibilities. You are to be accountable in many ways. One of the best ways to be accountable is to become a good learner. As you learn, you grow. As you grow in your Christian life, your love for your Savior and His church will grow. The Bible will help you discover new truths to live by. You will respect other Christians and seek to learn from them. You will grow through praying, giving, serving, and witnessing. God will help you to live more Christlike at home, school, church, and in your community. Your relationship to people around you should reflect that you are a Christian. Of course, we don't always succeed in having the best relations with others, but we should always be working at and learning how to love others as Christ did.

Why is it important that you be a responsible learner early in your Christian life? Think about these reasons.

1. Learning helps you grow in understanding of God. This is an excellent way to be responsible!
2. Learning can help you discover God's plan for your life. You are acting in a responsible way when you want to know what God's will is for your life.
3. Learning helps you know how to better serve others. God's Word can help us know how to love, forgive, and help others. When we know these things, we are growing as useful members of Christ's church.

How Do I Become a Christian?

You and This Book

So we've come to the end of this book. You have read it and have done the personal learning activities. In the beginning of this book, I told you why I was writing it. Do you remember? If not, flip back to the first page and reread the short introduction. That tells you why I wrote this book.

I hope that you have gained a better understanding of:

- the Bible as God's message of love to you;
- what it means to be lost and separated from God's forgiveness;
- that God planned for and sent Jesus to be your Savior;
- what you must do to accept Jesus as your Savior;
- what it means to join the church and follow God's will for your life.

Do you remember that I promised to pray for you? I have and I do. Even though I can't call you by name, I have prayed for you as a reader of this book. You know my name as author of this book. But God knows both of our names. That's what is important!

My greater hope is that, as you have journeyed through this book, you have discovered that you need to make your decision to trust Christ as Savior, perhaps with the help of some trusted friend in your life. If either of these two things are true, then my time writing has been well spent.

God bless you as you live your life each day.

Prayerfully yours,
Muriel Blackwell